Anatomy of a Warrior

How God Healed Me

Jennifer Mears

Edited by
Nicole Queen

VISION PUBLISHING
HOUSE

Contents

Introduction   v

1. The Purge   1
2. The Resurrection   9
3. The Little Girl in the Street   15
4. The Message   21
5. The Ministry   27
6. The Beginning   41

   Prayer of Encouragement   51
   Acknowledgments   53
   About the Author   57

Introduction

I did it. I took off the kid gloves and began to write my story. You know the one. *Ugh!* It's the one where the girl gets molested, raped, runs away, enslaved to fear, codependent on her abusers, locked into a mold that was never suited for her called religion, and hates herself until Jesus shows her love.

Yeah. *That* one.

Remember how she wanted to be liked so badly in school that rejection from bullies thrust her into bathroom stalls, where she devoured her stale lunch? Remember how just telling her story caused her so much grief that she'd taken the gloves on and off for decades, silently refusing to relive that pain?

But it was now or never.

See, *life happened.* She came home from prison, married the first joker who asked, and was impregnated with her first and only child. You know, her son—special needs, requiring a lot of care. She takes care of him all alone and does a good job (if you ask me), but she never gets around to living— because she is too afraid to.

Life squeezed her into a corner where she had to write her way out. Her son's needs require flexibility. Government assistance requires her to stay poor—or make enough to not need them anymore. She felt trapped. Day in and day out, she sat in her room, telling herself this narrative.

Yes, she prayed. But *faith without works is dead* (James 2:17). It was time for her to take action.

As I spoke with her, she glazed over with shame about her newly diagnosed, formerly misdiagnosed, mental illness, as if it disqualified her from owning her story somehow.

I called her a fraud.

She's not afraid of life with a mental illness. I heard she was wrongly diagnosed with bipolar disorder at age 16.

No.

She is afraid of feeling the pain that comes when the truth parts your lips. Afraid of owning the disgrace of needing so much grace. Afraid of humbly seeing her life for the miracle that it is.

She is a wife-in-training — mom *on fleek*— a *dunamis power woman* who cannot be beaten. And she *knows* it!

As I turn off my recorder and look her square in the eye, I refuse to permit her to continue as an imposter. Using *everything* to protect her, she's worse than Nino Brown. This girl's gotta own her truth. *Without hesitancy.*

Introduction

I like this girl, but I will not tolerate the lies—especially from people who lie to themselves.

I'm going to give her my two cents before I cut this mic and camera back on and let her decide for herself what is truth—the reality she's showing me, or what she's trying *not* to see.

* * *

Let me tell you something:

Not owning your power
Seeking permission to exist
A thing of your past
That you can't seem to resist

Keeping you safe from more pain
Or so you think
Jesus prayed for you
Remember the cup you must drink

Bear your cross
Life comes with pain
But it produces glory
Reclaim your name

Pain is not the end of your story
It was *necessary*
Just to get you to this
That feeling in your gut
You cannot dismiss

Listen to that little voice inside
The one that cries

Introduction

Feel those feelings
The good and the bad

Life is meant to be had
Enjoyed, experienced
This is *year forty*
Come on, Miss
Tell the real story

* * *

She broke down, her fingers threading through her thick, crinkly hair, stopping at the two gray strands on top.

"I am a compulsive liar," she whispered.

She lies to herself *every day* about what is possible—because when she does what she *knows* she can do, pain will inevitably come. And victimhood is safer than vulnerability.

Jesus.

She tried to tear up but shook it off quickly, knowing it was just another scheme. Squaring her shoulders, she spoke—and the troubled waters in her soul were quiet.

"I'd rather be a victim," she said, "and it be *your* fault, than to be vulnerable and it be *my own*. Or worse—nobody's fault. Just...life. I need someone to blame for all this pain."

"Oh, Jesus," she cried.

"I never accepted that *vulnerability is a choice. My* choice. And I *will* get hurt in the process. But if I never open myself up to the potential for pain... I *cannot* live."

"And that is how my life has been. Anesthetizing myself from pain. And my choice *not* to feel pain cut me off from life...until I met you," she said.

I thought this wouldn't be easy for her.

But once I called her bluff, she came clean—with herself and with God.

She said she was ready to acknowledge her hidden agenda—to live a pain-free life, as if she knew better than God.

As she opened up, looking back and forward, I recorded the details.

This.

This is the *anatomy* of a warrior.

Chapter 1

The Purge

"Ma'am," I said, "you had everyone fooled." See, I thought this was the story of a girl who had endured so much trauma and was afraid to be happy for fear that it'd all be taken away from her.

Oh boy, was I wrong!

Yes, you've endured great trauma... *yada yada yada*— it's been told a thousand times, in your life and in others. But what I can't get past is how many excuses you made to keep yourself miserable.

Well, misery does love company. So, God isolated me for eight years, slowly and surely chipping away at everything and everyone I leaned on as a crutch. Until I was left with the girl in the mirror.

And I still made excuses.

And I still told myself lies.

It's like I was waiting for someone to save me from me. Turns out, the Savior is Christ in me.

What were some of the lies you told yourself to keep you unhappy?
What are the ones that kept you from rising to your own standards, and
from having the peace and joy Jesus died for you to have?

1

The infamous "I'm not enough." Fear 101. "But my momma did this, and my daddy didn't do that."

Whenever something with the potential to challenge my painless life showed up, I defected to infancy, instability, and—well, you said it—misery.

What will you do differently now that you know that I know that you know you're not telling yourself the truth? Fear, self-induced anxiety, and depression are all lies!

Well, right now, I want to cuss and scream. I want to throw a fit because I've been *found out*. I want to ball up into a fetal position and suck my thumb.

But I'm *not* going to do that.

What I *will* do is take ownership.

I'm a little under two hundred pounds overweight. I own that. I'm ready to change that.

I have no income. That's my fault.

Yeah, I'm a special needs single mom, and it's been a struggle, but my lack of hustle? *That's on me.*

I *own* that.

I'm gifted in the arts, but haven't been selling my art to generate passive income. I *own* that.

I was a minister at my church until I had a psychotic breakdown, but that doesn't mean I can't minister ever again. I *own* that.

It's my fault if I let fear—which is my favorite lie—and control—which is my favorite habit and illusion—keep me from living the life of my dreams.

I *own* that.

My narrative is changing as we speak. I am the free woman because I choose to be free. There's too much life in me for me to walk around dead.

Pain didn't numb me; I numbed myself for fear of pain. I think a good start to wrapping my mind around *living* is to feel pain, since it's been my silent nemesis.

What hurts right now? Knowing a lot of this is my fault hurts. I just envisioned myself standing in a crack cocaine alley, a bleak abyss, with light on the other side of the street. And all I had to do was *walk out*. But I know that shaming myself for not taking responsibility is just another one of my card tricks.

I want to take responsibility for my actions and inactions, but not for the abuse. Abuse is never your fault.

You mentioned you were molested, raped, and a runaway. How does all that feel to you? You know... without the protective lies?

Dirty. And even dirtier.

Before I even knew I had an innocence, I was turned into a *sexbot*. Used. Cheap. Had. I didn't know it, but I feel like I'll never be pure again.

She began stroking her forehead from side to side— the saddest look in her eyes. It was as if she just *realized* what had happened to her. She needs to grieve:

- The loss of her childhood innocence
- The loss of her virginity
- But *not* her purity

Let's give her space to grieve. *Selah.*

How does it feel to be free? To process that age-old weight? I've been devastated so many times in life. I didn't even *realize* it until now. It should've killed me. But I didn't die. *No.*

Instead, I arose—with more determination to love and *be* loved. God in me is strong— stronger than hell. For every violation of my person that should've destroyed my self-worth and sense of self—God breathed upon it and taught me to love myself.

Each time the enemy reminds me of a pedophile or abuser who

took advantage of me, I see God's grace covering them and me. I stand in *awe* of the love of God for me.

What other junk do you need to be free of? Grief.

I lost a teammate.

I lost *myself* trying to overlook and excuse the failings of my teammate.

Essentially, within my short-lived, long-death of a marriage, there were two casualties.

Me.

And my husband.

Dang.

And my son.

I just realized the effect my broken marriage had on my developing little fetus and child.

So, I'm a Pinterest junky and on there I found a grief teardrop model:

T = *To accept the reality of loss*
E = *Experience the pain of the loss*
A = *Adjust to the new environment without the lost person*
R = *Reinvest in the new reality*

** *The Tear Drop Model was made using the Four Tasks of Mourning created by J. W. Worden.*

* * *

I've been frozen at *adjusting* to the loss. I never knew there was another step. That I had to reinvest in my life *without* the person.

This is yet another devastation I've survived.

I'm *done* with survival mode. I am ready to *reinvest* in the new reality of my life.

I'm forty. I have a special needs child in puberty. And I am dripping with gifts and abilities that I never considered using until now.

My experiences alone are priceless, as they could encourage and empower so many women.

What does reinvesting look like for you? It's honoring myself. It looks like honoring my feelings so that I won't lose one of the MVPs on the team, again. And learning to work with the other MVP on the team— the *Holy Spirit.* I love the Holy Spirit. We work well together. Even when there's a catastrophic emotional BOOM, He somehow gets me where I need to be.

Reinvesting in the new reality means going to work with what I have at my disposal right now. I'm anointed to teach, pray, and connect with God-influencing others to desire that connection. I'm naturally creative and gifted to compose all sorts of works of art.

Yes, it sounds like I'm on to something.

Indeed. I am designing a program for women in institutions to utilize the arts to purge and expose them to the gospel of grace. It is called Ifreewomen®.

How would you recommend other warriors purge?

Freely. Without judgment. No one knows or can tell you the right way to heal. It is relative to each warrior. You may feel like you are not healing because you are comparing your process to where you think you ought to be, not realizing how much progress you're making already.

Patiently. It's a process, a journey, a new life you're embarking upon. It takes time to release dead things so that you can live.

I asked her if she was ready—ready to live.

She let out a resounding yes, with tears in her eyes. "Yes! Yes! Yes!" she said. I've suffered, died—I've done everything, but live! The time is now.

Now, living is going to require some recalibration. She agreed. She'd been so accustomed to suffering and lying in her grave that she needed to learn how to push herself to live until it became a habit. She's a dreamer who never closed her eyes.

She never actualized or gave life to her dreams because it was too risky.

There was a short stint in her history where she dreamt, but then life happened, and she thought it was over.

Well, no more. Her dreams were hidden—beneath fears, doubts, *what ifs*, lack of resources, etc. Living requires dreaming. And they're both action words. She had to get up and take action.

She didn't know where to start. But she knew how to be curious. And she let her questions and desire to explore send her on a daring journey of discovery. Nothing was out of reach for her. Travel. Learning a new language. Shopping trips. A new look. Fitness goals.

She's about to start practicing smiling, too. She has a grin that went with the suffering. But it's time to start smiling—for real.

Sistalove, you betta smile. Stop waiting for everybody else to be happy, and *you* be happy. Believe. Yes. Life really can be good. After so much trauma, the love of God changes everything. *Life is good.*

* * *

My smile is jumping off of my face
I applaud and give You praise
You're not even finished, and I'm blown away
That You'd purpose to rebuild a heart
A life shattered and torn so far

Tears, my body aching from the pain
Bottled inside, devastated. I held the loss dear
But Jesus Messiah, my Great Physician
Healing me in Your closed incubator
Feeding me through tubes
Father God, You're my great heart regulator

As I'm dependent on You—You're my respirator
You heal things I didn't even know were broken
This time with You is where destiny meets
The death of the old me, and the authentic me is open

Anatomy of a Warrior

Every word that should have been spoken
That I didn't utter for fear, I braved the silence
And I speak clear. I take on awkward pauses
And cross-eyed glances

I stand up to demons that have had too many chances
Power of God, rise up in me
Holy resuscitator
Let me walk on the heights as bold as bold can be

Let all men know that I've been with Thee
Let hell shake and demons tremble
At the mention of Your name

Thy Kingdom come
Thy will be done, again and again
May multitudes be added to the body of Christ
To continuously give You praise

Glory, Honor, Majesty
Is due Your Name

Chapter 2

The Resurrection

"I just don't wanna have another psychotic breakdown," she exclaimed. "It was mortifying to be outside of myself in front of the whole church assembly."

"You have a severe mental illness?"

"Yes!"

"Okay, so what?"

"So what, what?" she quickly retorted, shifting back and forth from anger to shame.

Perhaps this is more reason for you to be gentle and vulnerable with yourself and people rather than a reason to recluse. Could it be that this is not the nail in the coffin but the light of resurrection?

"I mean, sis, how many people do you know who can comfort someone in pain like you?"

"Actually," she said, "that reminds me of when I used to volunteer in the prisons and jails for about eight years." I'd always say, *I don't want them to feel like how I felt in that situation.* Correction—I don't know what I felt in that situation exactly. I just know that I was in pain, and I didn't want anyone else to go through it without knowing and loving themselves like I did."

I felt alone. My ministry was more about keeping the company of the suffering than anything else and providing them hope. I probably wouldn't have relapsed on marijuana (street and medical), alcohol, and sin altogether if I had allowed myself to be comforted the way I sought to comfort others.

My psychotic breakdown was scripted. I'd spent years trying to be the perfect single parent to my son— watching his father act as if he never had a child, in the same church. I underutilized my gifts and abilities and put all my hope into people to rescue me from me. My resentment and emotional pain grew to an unbearable amount.

The mounting pressure of bills, blame, and loads of shame erupted one sweet day in March of 2022. It was an avalanche. It was clear from Neptune that I was headed for destruction. I stepped away from God, gave in to every sinful desire I had, and one day a voice told me to stop taking my medicine."

"Game over."

"The beauty is the mystery of Jesus Christ. When I stepped away from God, He stepped even closer to me."

"When I invited men into my bedroom, Jesus clung tightly to me. The Holy Spirit tugged on my heart when I wouldn't return to Christ. God had the troubled *man-boy* I was sleeping with confess that I deserved better. He kept rejecting me and treating me badly until I began to believe it for myself."

"God moved through a sinful, lustful, evil relationship while I was bound by the enemy, seemingly unreachable, to get my attention. I changed gears, but evil spirits still had a hold on me. I tried to purge my house, but my heart was still wrongfully devoted."

"Worse, the voices and images kept following me. I was psychotic in seminary. But there was something specific about these demons that followed me around and talked to me. They hated God and the church."

One thing I know about myself is that I love God and the church.

"These spirits were hallucinations and delusions, but they weren't benign—they were sent by Satan. Here I sat in seminary, trying to do what I thought was the will of God for my life, tormented by evil spirits."

"To this day, I never stopped to consider the power of God at work in me until now."

She sighed.

"What do you mean?"

"I mean, I've been looking at this all wrong."

"I've been to hell. Seen the demons. And Jesus Christ fought for me to overcome them. The Holy Spirit in me is greater than the hellions I've seen. There is no evil spirit that can dominate me. No power in hell that can torment me. God in me is greater. I know this experientially. No one could get me out of the hell I was in but God. He wasn't external to me—it was the power of God inside of me. His Spirit was still working for me despite my failing.

My God, my God, *how great Thou art!*"

She let out a deep sigh of relief and said, "I just got my strength! I just found my power!"

This newfound power is Christ in me, the hope of glory. I am learning to rely on and release this power. My coworker is all-knowing, all-present, and all-powerful. His strength is made perfect in my weakness."

Now I view my weaknesses as strengths—you know, the schizoaffective disorder, social awkwardness, and my other nuanced brain-teasers of a personality. If I could be strong—if I could be strong in Him—then I can stand up out of this grave.

Yes. This grave is where I have pillows and comforter blankets.

Yes. I resurrect from this place of discounting myself because of my mental illness and other challenges.

A warrior uses everything at their disposal, including things that look weak. It's the weak things that are the most effective because they catch the enemy off guard. The Holy Spirit has taught me that His power in me is great, and I need not fear.

What has stopped you from resurrecting in the past, and what will keep you resurrected in the present? Indubitably, it was fear and pride and shame and guilt. But the major culprit was fear under them all.

See, what I didn't know was that investing involves risk.

Fear paralyzes and promotes risk reduction or elimination.

Having a mental illness and being publicly humiliated was, in fact, a public display of God's grace. However, I didn't always view it that way.

I felt like, because I had a mental illness and other flaws, I might as well play dead. It is risky to be graced by God—misunderstood by some and condemned by others. In grade school, before I dropped out and hit the streets, I was treacherously bullied. It was there that I first learned to play dead. I call it depression.

On the other hand, in my family of origin, I learned to talk fast and loud to feel heard and seen. I remember having all sorts of dreams—sci-fi fantasy types that involved the past and my take on future events. Something like mania. The bullies and my family dynamic didn't make me schizoaffective, but they contributed to the way I developed.

I remember being codependent in elementary school. Obsessing about people liking me. I had two close girlfriends. I remember telling one that another girl, much younger, liked me—as if I'd somehow arrived.

Post-resurrection, I can see what kept me in the grave so long.

Me.

The fear of *me*.

Who I was kept me from becoming who I am and who I could be.

As for what will keep me out of the grave, it's an intimate knowledge of God.

The knowledge of the goodness of the Lord—His love for me—is why I am where I am today and why I will remain.

"The beautiful thing about dying and being resurrected is that you get up with power," she said.

Now her focus isn't on *not* having another psychotic breakdown.

No!

But rather, operating in the Spirit at such a level that she experiences breakthroughs—to the point that she blesses others exponentially.

This warrior's eyes are fixed on Christ. She loves God and His people. She now understands that God uses her weakness—the mental illness, her pain, and her grief—as a platform. He shines His light of glory through her cracks. Her anatomy is vulnerable, and God gets all the glory.

That is an invitation to put your full confidence in God. To see Him work miracles—unimaginable endings that look nothing like the beginnings. You are inviting her to be intimately blessed and to know You for who You are—God Almighty, who can do anything—if she just believes.

So, You send out an invitation to her. Yes, Lord, she says. I accept Thee offer. I will trust You.

Chapter 3

The Little Girl in the Street

I met a little girl in the street
Matted hair and dirty feet
Eyes downturned in shame
Muted, unable to speak
Terrified, neglected, nothing to eat
Traumatized, disrespected—she was weak
Our eyes met just for a moment
Trying to ignore her
I hurried by, unwilling to help
This little girl followed me
I went on with my day
As if I never saw her
But oh boy, did she see me
Every time I looked up
Her eyes were on me
As if I had something to give
Anxious, I ran down a street
To escape this miniature beast
It ended in death

Jennifer Mears

Looking to the right
I couldn't turn left
I was uncomfortable
And I wanted to fight or flee
From this little girl
Who kept following me
Who was she
And what did she want
Finally, we locked eyes
This time, I tried to take an interest
But every time I saw her
I felt intense anger
Didn't she know better
Than to put herself in danger
Couldn't she fend for herself
In this cold, cold world
Why couldn't she be like
Other little girls
Why wasn't she normal
Why was she so hard to love
A star would fall from heaven
Before she'd be worthy of my love
This victimized, traumatized
Dirty little girl
Opened her mouth
And out came the world
She spoke of abuse
She spoke of great struggle
She spoke of horrendous sights
How people muzzled
Her with their cruel hatred
And bitterness
Until she could take it no more
She said she'd been following me

Because she could take the pain no more
She said she sought love
She said she wanted to live
She said she needed to be heard
And that she had nothing to give.
But the love she receives
Would grow her up
The love she only dreamt of
If she refused to give up
To get to me
She'd stepped through fire
To get to me
She'd been through storms
To get to me
She had to fight
She knew once we spoke
I'd do what was right
And love her
Because *she is I*
Of weakness and wonder
My alibi

Owning my power while being compassionate with myself is vulnerability. It makes me the most authentic *me*. I need my compassion because of what I've gone through, and my power to go through. That's what makes me a warrior.

I can walk in my power and feel my feelings. I can do anything. Learning to stand on what is trying to swallow me up, hold me down, or consume me is not easy. If it were, *everyone* would be walking on water.

But there's something about this little girl that I met in the street. A resilience. A determination. An inner resolve. Surely God placed it there. Surely God is keeping her, having endowed her with supernatural strength.

But what if the *strongest* thing she could do right now is be *weak*? What if her power lies in resting in His arms? Laying herself bare and surrendering to Someone much greater than she?

There's beauty in being kept.

What if the only way to walk in my power is to release?

Allowing the joints and muscles in my legs and knees to collapse.

Falling into grace.

That's it.

She must trust God enough to let go, trusting that upon her release, He is able—willing—to catch her. And not just any catch—but hold her.

Hold me now, Lord, she prays. Not realizing that she is so frightened and wounded that she won't allow His presence close.

Intimate trust is required to be held. There's a letting go that must happen for the person being held.

The image that comes to mind is someone deeply hurt and wounded, who *needs* the Lord to come near but, out of fear, tries to control the moment—unwilling to let go.

Oh, Jesus.

I have chronic, unexplained pain in my back, pelvis, and joints, and chronic migraines. I take the prescribed medication, but it simply masks the pain—and only for a moment.

I've noticed that I brace myself for the pain, tensing the muscles in my butt and back, making the pain unbearable.

Honestly, I don't know how much pain I'm in, or how much pain I'm causing by trying to control pain.

What do you think would happen if you took a deep breath and allowed the Lord to touch you—right there, as you are hurting?

"I'm scared to let Him touch it—*me*. I fear that He cannot make it better. Since I blame Him for the pain, I don't trust Him to relieve it."

Do you think you can trust Him to comfort you in your pain anyway? Say it *is* His fault. Will you allow Him to comfort you despite that?

Could an all-seeing, all-knowing, all-powerful God allow your pain...

And comfort you in the same breath?
Is He able to inflict wrath and bring good?
Does He bless and curse?
Can He be trusted to judge and to acquit?
Is Jesus proof that the Father is able to do both?

Didn't He permit the fall of man— and then send the Son of Man?
Isn't He Lord of all?

That means pain and pleasure, harm and healing—are His.
Breakthrough moment. This is your breakthrough moment, Woman of God. Realizing that God is worthy of your trust.
Yes, He allowed you to be afflicted— but He is waiting *patiently,* *ready* to comfort you. He will heal you in His time. Some pain may remain. But know this. God can be trusted with your pain.

Let Him in, Jennifer.
Let the Lord touch your mortal body
And remove the stain of sin and shame
Autocorrect, by virtue of His Majesty
All that is askew
Realign you with grace
Let Him help you

She sideswiped her quilted two-strand twist
With a look in her eyes that said it all
Could this be? she thought
Can I trust God
Could this be my moment
To hand over the keys to my soul
Can I finally—at once—release control

Jennifer Mears

Is there Someone greater than I
Who can handle me and my baggage
I can let go
I will let go
That's it, warrior
Daily
Moments in between moments
Let go

Chapter 4

The Message

The greatest crime of her life was that she was made to distrust what was on the inside of her. She tiptoed through life, waiting for others to validate or approve of her, constantly feeling the need to prove herself to others.

Here lies the message: the criminals broke in. Criminals only come to steal where there is a treasure. She never had to prove she was treasure—the presence of criminals did that for her. She needed only to believe it.

All of the anxiety and fear she felt throughout her forty years in emotional and spiritual captivity, God has brought to an end. She told me how amazed she was that she could read the Bible most of her life and miss the big picture.

In Genesis, a criminal stepped on the scene to convince God's treasured creatures, Eve and Adam, that they had something to prove. He tricked them into trying to prove that God was good with crafty words of deception. He tempted them by appealing to their appetite —an area of vulnerability. And in their pride they tried to meet their own needs.

They fell.

He tried the same thing with Jesus in the wilderness.

Sanctimoniously, she attended worship service year after year, wondering why nothing changed. Until Christ touched her heart.

After the breakdown—which was public for all to see—she clung to self-will and despair. She let herself go, literally. She stopped caring for her physical appearance and took no interest in life, not knowing that hidden within her fragile clay jar was treasure. She was carrying costly oil in the spiritual realm.

See, God had preserved her. Yes. Through it all. The shaming, naming, defaming. Through every high and every low.

It was Jesus Christ, the Messiah, who wouldn't let her go. Tucked deep inside her was His Spirit. He used her special needs son and his unruly behavior to push the real from the counterfeit. The warrior from within.

The evil spirit that loomed in her son provoked her sorely. He tormented her daily. He defied God in her, and it vexed her spirit. She didn't know what to do. So, she began to fast.

Her son grew worse—having public outbursts and meltdowns, fits of violence, spitting, and rage. The intensity grew to a boiling point. She found herself in the emergency room with her son after one public episode just before Christmas. Fasting, praying, seeking the Lord. She needed to separate the diagnosis from the demon and wage war. Medication changes were made. Some improvement. But that spirit still tormented her.

I'm reminded of Hannah and Peninnah, who tormented her until Hannah wept bitterly and made a vow to the Lord. She was vulnerable and humble and took action in all humility.

It was enough.

Hannah vowed to give her son back to God. She knew God would give her a son, and she was devoted in vulnerability to give him back to the Lord. The warrior we've been discussing in this book had a decision to make.

Will she let go and give her son back to the Lord? Will she proclaim, "Thy Master's will be done; not my will, but Thine!"

God is speaking to the warrior, beckoning her anatomy of vulnerability. The message she hadn't received was the one she wasn't willing to hear: that it is time to let go of her one and only son.

Lord, she said, "I need something to hold onto."

"Here I am," says the Lord, "hold on to Me."

Up until now, all she had held onto was anxiety, which is emotional manipulation. It's a quest to keep from feeling vulnerable. It defies God.

The heart palpitations she felt. The invisible hand around her throat. The feeling in the pit of her stomach. Her hurried speech. Her inability to think clearly.

See, her brain was overpowered with what might go wrong if she didn't control everything in her environment to prevent harm. She was in sin, and she knew it.

Leaving her son's doctor's appointment, she had a full-blown panic attack. That was the norm for those appointments—but this one was the worst. This time, she watched herself get hit by a bus. A bus that she was driving. *Because she had to be in control!*

This is the genesis of the revelation:

- She learned in childhood to try to control her mother's anger.
- She feared her mother's anger sorely, and it damaged her ability to be vulnerable.
- She learned to control her mother's anger by pleasing and performing, living in constant fear and dread.
- She never expressed her emotions for fear that it might anger someone.
- Always walking on eggshells. Never telling the truth about how she felt or being authentic.

We go through life not realizing how interconnected the details of the events of our lives are. How I show up at my son's doctor's appointment is directly related to how I felt as a small child.

Generational curses are being broken here and now because how I show up today—and moving forward—is directly related to how my son and generations to come after me will show up.

The message is this: When you are afraid and you desperately need someone or something to hold onto— hold onto God. When Jesus was on the cross, in great pain and suffering, as vulnerable as vulnerable can be—He needed someone to hold on to— to cry out to.

Three statements from the cross come to mind:

1. "My God, My God, why have You forsaken Me?"
2. "Into Your hands, I commend My Spirit."
3. "It is finished."

In whatever state you find yourself:

- Feeling forsaken? Hold on to God.
- Fully surrendered, ready to transition? Hold on to God.
- Finished the assignment? Hold on to God.

That's what she thought she needed to do. Just hold on to God. But then came the most blatant revelation: She didn't have to be in control anymore. Or hold onto God. Because God was holding onto her.

In awestruck amazement, she declared: "God is so good that He let me hold onto Him for dear life—until I learned how to be held."

* * *

Anatomy of a Warrior

Father God,

Thank You for the real message—
That I have nothing to fear because You are in control.

That I don't have to live in fear of human anger
Or try to control my environment in anxiety.

Teach my muscle membranes to release every care to You.
As I surrender.

As I forget what the last 40 years of bondage have taught me

And lay hold of truth.
I do so, held by You.

In Jesus' name, Amen.

Chapter 5

The Ministry

She returned to church in 2022 with so much shame and inner confusion, having been sat down as a minister, which brought about much grief—grief she never spoke of. She told me she kept it in her body and carried it around day and night. It ached. This, coupled with the pre-existing pain of her unhealed trauma and the tension she carried in her back in the form of spasms, was too much to bear.

This girl was hurting.

She would become vulnerable with the Lord, but when pain or fear arose, she would take control. Her anatomy was inconsistent with the Lord's purposes when she refused to be weak.

But God had a plan.

Using evil from all directions—uncertainty, her limitations, and her mental illness—the Holy Spirit gently guided the warrior to be vulnerable more consistently. To lean on God for support in any and every circumstance. Total dependence. To admit that she didn't have all the answers and be okay with that. To take off the armor and stop protecting herself with her devices. To be led by the Holy Spirit.

This was essential because she was called by God to full-time ministry, to a life of fellowship with the Spirit, to intimacy with the God-head on new levels.

"Instead, God chose things the world considers foolish in order to shame those who think they are wise. And he chose things that are powerless to shame those who are powerful. 28 God chose things despised by the world, things counted as nothing at all, and used them to bring to nothing what the world considers important." 1 Corinthians 1:27-28

"What stands out to you in the text?" I asked the warrior. "How God chooses! He wants the ones deemed foolish, the powerless, and those considered nothing at all."

Vulnerable.

She couldn't go into ministry until she learned this lesson. Indeed, she had completed ministerial training seven years prior. She had also received revelation from God in the form of a dream during that same period—that the elders of the church would call for her, that she would be greatly used by God, and that she needed to let her son go.

Now, seven years later—the number of completion, totality, and perfection in biblical numerology—it is the appointed time. She is about to be thrust into her role and assignment in the church.

Now, in 2025, she is ready.

God has healed her troubled soul from years of trauma and abuse. She's made amends for the harm she's caused to others and received forgiveness from God, others, and herself. She has learned spiritual discipline—how to fast, paying close attention to what she allows to go out and what she allows into her spirit, and how to pray. She's forgiven those who have hurt her deeply.

Most importantly, she's full of the Holy Spirit.

As she speaks with me regarding all the progress she's made in the Lord, there's one area where she feels she still needs to grow: fear.

She is a leader and a visionary, but fear holds her back. She believes she would see more results in her son as well if she weren't so afraid.

She just realized something. There's more in her than she realizes. In the moment, when it is time to rise up—she will. She's already on the ascent. She can say "No" and communicate her needs in a healthy way without fear, whereas before, she would just comply.

I think what she's tripping over is that she's watching herself grow, and she may be demanding perfection—which is not an option. She may also think that because she felt fear, it's a sign of defeat.

Or, because she didn't ace it every time, she's not making sufficient progress in that area.

God is ready to bless you and move you into an area of influence. He is confident in you. Be confident in yourself. Christ in you can't lose.

She prepared her heart with more fasting and seeking the Lord. God kept her in His spiritual incubator—not permitting outside influences in or allowing her to get out while He put the finishing touches on her healing.

Meanwhile, she began to realize just how in sync she was with the Holy Spirit. It was uncanny and a little exciting at first.

Then she realized how serious this was.

This was Kingdom.

God would lead her somewhere in prayer and study, and then the following service, the bishop would be preaching from that very subject. Her life, where God had her, would directly align with the Word of God. She was in tune with what the Spirit of the Lord was saying to the church on any given Sunday.

She sat out of ministry for about two and a half years—learning to care for herself and her son.

Learning what love is.

Healing.

It was now time to have her ministerial license reinstated.

During the time she sat out, while she grappled with vulnerability, she would write sermons, study the Word, and commune with God.

Her greatest and fastest growth spurt happened during the

winter of 2024 into January 2025. It was like things were happening at lightning speed.

God was working the entire time, but this was when she couldn't help but notice it.

Things that would've once wiped her out, she shrugged off. Sometimes, it may have taken a second or two, but she bounced back. In vulnerability, that warrior grew. Her anatomy is proof.

She wrote a sermon called "Who He Is." God had her write it in preparation for her return to ministry:

Sermon: Who He Is

God's eternal plan is to show us who He is—Love, Perfect Love.

Vulnerable, even to the point of death. To do that, He chose to use evil to reveal His great love for us. We cannot escape God, and we need not fear the darkness because light and darkness are the same to Him (Psalm 139:11-12).

We're just as vulnerable in the light as we are in the dark, and God's presence is with us no matter where we find ourselves.

Vulnerability Defined

Vulnerability is being open to attack, danger, and harm:

- It means not going around trying to protect ourselves with defense mechanisms.
- It means surrendering control to God.
- It means accepting our weaknesses and limitations, letting the Holy Spirit lead, and being amazed at the results.

The Lamb of God Is Vulnerable

From the very beginning, Jesus was vulnerable:

- In Revelation 12, we see Jesus as the child whom the dragon seeks to devour as the woman gives birth to Him.
- In Matthew 2:13-14, an angel warns Joseph in a dream to flee to Egypt with the Child until further notice because Herod seeks to destroy Him.

Being fully God and fully man, Jesus Christ experienced vulnerability in its fullest measure. As perfect man, He was vulnerable in His humanity. As perfect God, He was powerful yet misunderstood —making Him vulnerable in His divinity.

As a child, Jesus experienced the vulnerability of human existence:

- As a young boy, He stayed behind after the Feast of the Passover in Jerusalem while His family unknowingly traveled ahead.
- Days passed before His parents realized He was missing.
- When they found Him, He was in the temple, listening and asking questions among the teachers.
- His parents were distraught, yet He submitted to them as a vulnerable child, growing in wisdom and stature (Luke 2:52).

But Jesus' vulnerability didn't end in His youth, as some might think. His very nature is vulnerable.

Love is vulnerable:

- The Holy Spirit led Jesus into the wilderness, where He was tempted by the devil.
- The tempter came to Him at His weakest moment—when He was hungry after fasting forty days and forty nights.
- Yet, Jesus overcame the devil's temptation.
- He didn't use physical strength, intellect, or human wisdom to resist.
- He relied completely on God the Father.

Because Jesus was willing to be vulnerable, He came out of the wilderness full of the Spirit and ready for His mission. The devil tempted Him to prove He was God through His own strength, but instead, Jesus chose to depend on the Father.

Jesus is vulnerable.

Jesus is perfect love.

Jesus is strength beyond measure.

Vulnerability in Jesus' Earthly Ministry

The undeniable vulnerability and compassionate love of God were on grand display for the world to see.

- Multitudes thronged Jesus.
- A woman touched His garment and was healed.
- He healed 10 lepers, the lame, and the blind.
- He taught about the Kingdom of Heaven.

Even Jesus' teaching was vulnerable:

- He spoke in parables that had no meaning to those with darkened understanding.
- His authority was constantly challenged by the chief priests and scribes.
- He was scrutinized and misunderstood.
- Jesus was vulnerable when He raised Lazarus from the dead.
- He needed God to help Him reveal to the people that He had been sent by the Father.
- It was this miracle that led the Pharisees to plot His death (John 11:53).

Jesus knew what was coming.

- In John 17, He prayed, "Father, the hour has come."
- The silent, vulnerable cry of "Daddy, I need You."
- He prayed that we would be one—as He and the Father are one (John 17:21).

To be one with Him requires intimacy. *Vulnerability.*

Jesus' Final Vulnerability

- Jesus was betrayed.
- Jesus was arrested.
- Jesus was innocent and sinless, yet He was sentenced to death.

From the throne of Heaven to Mary's womb, from the cross to His resurrection, Jesus remained vulnerable.

Even now, as He prepares to return for His Church, He is still vulnerable—because He is Love.

Will you be vulnerable?

- Will you give Him your heart today?
- How about your soul?
- How about your life?
- Will you stop relying on yourself to figure it all out and let Him take control?

Jesus made Himself vulnerable for you.

The Kingdom of God Is Vulnerable

Today, I'm calling out to those who have been sitting in church for years—week after week, month after month, year after year.

Same bills.
Same struggles.
Same issues.
Nothing shifting in the spiritual realm.
Not expecting much.

Maybe you've seen some progress, but deep down, something is telling you: there has to be more. And there is. It is found in vulnerability.

- When we surrender and allow ourselves to be weak before God.
- When we admit we don't have it all together.

- When we rend our hearts, not just our garments (Joel 2:13).

God is after our hearts, not our religious performances. But here's the problem in the body of Christ today:

Too many armor-protected, self-elected, unbelieving so-called believers.

- We haven't seen a biblical miracle in how long?
- Why? Because we refuse to be vulnerable.
- We don't truly believe God, risk persecution, or fast and pray until something happens.
- We won't come together in love and unity—because we're too busy protecting ourselves from each other.

Instead, we create cliques where we control the narrative, minimize the risk, or isolate ourselves altogether.

But ask yourself this: How did Jesus look on the cross?

- Was He in control, or was He fully surrendered?
- I struggled with this because He's God—He had to be in control.
- But He chose surrender.

Think about that. Didn't He command us to take up our cross and follow Him (Luke 9:23)?

God is moving in His church, but this next move is not for the proud, the self-reliant, or the comfortable. This move is for those willing to die to themselves.

The Kingdom Belongs to the Vulnerable

Jesus said,

> Let the children come to me. Don't stop them! For the Kingdom of Heaven belongs to those who are like these children.

> — Matthew 19:14-15 (NLT)

Why children? Because children are vulnerable. And we are God's sons and daughters.

> Creation is eagerly waiting for God to reveal who His children really are.

> — Romans 8:19 (NLT paraphrased)

Something happened in most of our childhoods that taught us vulnerability was too much of a risk:

- Maybe it was an absent parent.
- Maybe it was rejection—feeling like you didn't belong.
- Maybe you were touched inappropriately, and you never felt safe emotionally.
- Maybe you were abused, and you never healed.
- Maybe nobody ever told you it was okay to love yourself.
- Maybe you did everything right, but nobody noticed. They only saw your flaws.

Could you live with that?
Who taught you fear?
Who made you feel insecure?
Who taught you doubt?

Who made you work for their approval?
Who made you feel unworthy of love?

A person may come to mind because of their actions—but Satan is the real enemy. Satan refused to be vulnerable before God.

He was consumed by pride, deceiving himself into thinking he could ascend above the Almighty.

 For you said to yourself, 'I will ascend to heaven and set my throne above God's stars. I will preside on the mountain of the gods, far away in the north.

— Isaiah 14:13 (NLT)

And in the church today, we see the same thing.

Christians Who Have Ascended Above God

How do we do this?

- When we don't seek Him first (Matthew 6:33).
- When we aren't led by His Spirit.
- When we have church without Him.
- When we let tradition, culture, family, fear, stress, and worldly trends dictate our response to God.

Consequentially, for some of us, it will take devastation to wake us up. But for others, a word from the Lord will be enough. *Which will you be?*

The Call to Vulnerability

Whether God allows you to be broken or whether you receive the Word today strip yourself of yourself:

- That little bit of you you're holding onto.
- Or for some, that whole bunch of you.

Let it go. Be vulnerable. God is vulnerable. We, as His church, must be vulnerable too. The Lamb of God is vulnerable—the most vulnerable. The Kingdom of God is vulnerable.

The move of God we are praying for will come through us—but only if we are willing to be vulnerable. The world needs to believe that Jesus was sent by God. But they won't believe it until we, His people, become one in Him—vulnerable.

* * *

Let's pray:

Lord, without vulnerability, there is no salvation. Without salvation, there is no hope for Your kingdom. We know we serve a victorious God, the Champion of all.

Lord, You could've defeated sin and Satan with brute force, but You didn't. You chose to let hell loose on earth and surrender Your own Son to die in vulnerability for the people.

What a grand display of Your love, restraint, and power. True power isn't force. True power is strength under control—under the Holy Spirit's control. True power is submitted and surrendered to the Lord.

Father, it is then and only then that we will see the devil flee from us. He's not running because we're not submitting as a people. But this word was brought today to inaugurate an appeal. This word is changing the tide in the body of Christ. Sons and daughters, and new converts, will throw away their old ideas, systems, beliefs, and devices that kept them from being vulnerable.

Creation is waiting for the sons and daughters of God to be revealed. No longer will we speak to a thing, and it not move. No longer will we live with something that You've already given us victory over. No longer will we be plagued by evil spirits—on the job or at home—because we don't have the power to remove them.

We're going to be vulnerable like You, Jesus. You have already given us the victory.

Father, cut through our generations of self-reliance, pride, and fear, and teach us to be vulnerable. Any opposition that would try to hinder this move in the church—we collectively bind it in the heavens, as it is bound on the earth.

In the matchless name of Jesus, we pray, Amen.

Chapter 6

The Beginning

Shaken out of her sleep at 3:45 a.m., she rolled over and glanced at her iPad to check the time. Why was she up so early? Her son didn't need to get ready for school for another 2 ½ hours.

It was God. He provoked her to pray. The Holy Spirit reminded her of the state of affairs in her life. She was in crisis. The demonic spirit in her son caused him to write 666 on the bathroom mirror, with the steam from the shower, have public outbursts, and be defiant and combative. His behavior worsened with time, and he was taking so many medications.

The warrior's life had become so small. She couldn't go shopping for fear that he would refuse to leave the mall or supermarket. He was 160 lbs., as tall as her, and untamable. He would often dart into traffic and try to elope.

The warrior would try to restrain him to keep him safe from oncoming traffic, but she wasn't physically strong enough to keep this up. She feared for his safety. The demonic spirit controlled church outings as well, with loud outbursts and violent behavior, defying her and refusing to obey.

She had a revelation. It was the beginning of answered prayer.

That morning, at 4:54 a.m., she prayed for mercy. She cried out to God in bitter tears and anguish, pleading for relief from the oppression of this demon in her son. She told God that she no longer wanted to be controlled by this spirit and that she surrendered her son, herself, and the situation to Him.

As she spoke to me, her countenance changed. She sat up in her seat, victory aglow on her face. She realized that the fear that plagued her life was the fuel this demon ran on. The spirit was only able to control her and undermine her authority because of her fear.

She knew that if she put her full and complete trust in God—depending totally on Him, letting go of the need to control her son in fear, and trusting God for deliverance—she would experience victory.

"Yes, Lord!" she resounded. She realized that the fear that plagued her life was the fuel this demon ran on. Perfect love casts out fear (1 John 4:18). She couldn't cast out the demon with fear.

This warrior had been saying, "In the name of Jesus, I command you to come out!" to this demon for at least four years.

She had tried everything: begging, pleading, pleasing, avoiding, denying, lying, manipulating (which is witchcraft). But never love.

What will it be like to completely trust God's love?

Phew! I just had a vision of a well-swept house. Clean on the inside. Organized. There will be no place for fear or unclean things to hide. She had tried everything. But never love.

Relying on this vulnerable love to remove the fear inside me, then being free enough and vulnerable enough to remove the spirit in my son, is just the beginning.

God is about to do miracles in our lives. Miracles, signs, and wonders—for His glory, to add to His kingdom daily, she said confidently. I agreed.

It was lonely fighting this fight. Family and friends didn't seem to understand. But God was okay with the loneliness—because He was right by her side. Indeed, living within her, empowering her every second of every day to be the warrior she has become.

Jesus knew loneliness. He was thronged by multitudes, but His ministry was hallmarked by Him constantly pulling away to commune with the Father in prayer—alone.

Even within His group of disciples, He had a small circle that was closer than the others. And during those final hours, when He suffered for the sins of the world, He was all alone on the cross of Calvary.

"How does that truth resonate with you?" I asked. She swept her now bone-straight hair to the side with a gleam in her eyes and said: "Well, that was always my problem. I grew up in a culture of codependency. I never believed that I could do anything meaningful on my own. And for God to call me and tell me the exact opposite—was quite the culture shock.

For years, I resisted the Holy Spirit's gentle arrest because I wanted to bring everybody and my momma with me on my journey. That is why I have made such progress in these past few months.

I left everybody behind, and my momma, and journeyed with the Lord. I implemented my boundaries. I said "NO!" I was led by the Spirit into the unknown—and it has been amazing. And to think this is only the beginning.

Codependency is ugly. Essentially, it is idolatry—a fear of doing things with just you and God. The behaviors are compulsive, and the lies told by Satan are unending, but the truth stops him in his tracks.

Fear is a lie. So, he said, "I heard Your voice in the garden, and I was afraid because I was naked; and I hid myself" (Genesis 3:10 NLT).

The first time fear is mentioned in the Bible is after man sinned. And what was Adam doing? Hiding. Protecting himself from himself, God, and his significant other. That is the objective of fear—every time.

We know from the Word of God that God has not given us the

spirit of fear (2 Timothy 1:7). So, if God didn't give it to us, where did it come from? It started with someone—Satan. He is the father of lies.

Fear is a lying spirit:

- It boasts of the worst-case scenario.
- It isolates.
- It dominates.
- It deceives.
- It seeks to control and bind.

But it is a lie.

That was the beginning. Nestled in the creation story is the Fall of Man. But there was another Man—a Man mentioned in Genesis 3:15. That Man is Jesus. He stood up where Adam fell down. Jesus sacrificed His life for our sins. He defeated Satan by vulnerably dying for all mankind and then rising with all power in His hands.

The liar, Satan, roams the earth pretending he's not defeated, that our sins aren't forgiven, and that we still have something to fear. But Jesus Christ proved His love for us on Calvary. There is nothing the devil can do to harm us. There is nothing God has not already done to save us. Yet, knowing this fact, I still wrestle with fear.

She grew silent. She realized—had she not resisted God, what took seven years could've been accomplished much sooner. She sighed with a melancholy grin.

"Well, I learned to trust Him."

"You know—to know what you know!" she said, her eyebrows arching in emphasis.

Speaking of trust, what are you trusting God for exactly? That's the beauty of being vulnerable. I'm trusting God for everything. But specifically—my business.

God spoke to me and laid a business venture on my heart. The name of my company is Immanuel Health Services LLC, and it provides direct support services to the developmentally disabled population receiving waivers through the DDA. It was truly divine the way God did this.

I was unemployed for a long time—in part because of my son and his needs/behavior, in part because of my own mental health needs, and largely because God was working on me. Anyway, I was insecure about not having my own income.

Everything I had was given to me—furniture, clothing, etc. While I was grateful, admittedly, I was insecure. Eventually, I learned to be content with where I was, and I appreciated God more for what I had. I became even more grateful for all the time I had at my disposal.

My son was receiving services through the DDA Family Supports Waiver, and direct support professionals would come into the home to provide care for him daily.

This went on for a while. There was a high turnover rate with staff, my son's behaviors were beginning to make staffing impossible, and the quality of staff being sent out was below our standards of care.

One day, a staff member was with my son. He was getting frustrated with him because my son was not listening—which was a regular occurrence between my son and staff. He would only listen to me—and even that was short-lived—hence the need for deliverance.

I was in my bedroom with the door cracked while they were in the living room. I heard the staff member say that if my son didn't sit down, he was going to spank him out of frustration. I told the staff he needed to leave.

Then, I prayed to God and said, "God, if only You could send us a staff like me." Mind you—I'd been unemployed for seven years. Then God gave me the revelation: I could be my son's staff. So, I went through the process and was hired by the agency as his direct support professional. My first job in ages.

I now see what God was doing in the spirit—isolating me with my son and the spirit so that I would be forced to rely on Him and see how His power would work through me to remove the unclean, evil spirit out of my son.

But God didn't stop there. As the job progressed, bills mounted. God gave me the idea for the business: Immanuel Health Services LLC. As the CEO, I will hire direct support professionals, as well as a manager and supervisor.

I am a new small business owner. Many details are unknown as of now. I sometimes feel like I can't do it or a fear of failure. But my faith is not in me. It is in the Lord.

Presently, I am awaiting approval of my DDA Provider application, which I submitted in October 2024. I'm vulnerable in the wait.

Trusting God is critical in everything I do. For instance, when I launch the business and begin making revenue—when I start receiving a salary—I will no longer qualify for the government housing program, Medical Assistance, or DDA support. That is scary.

That was my initial reaction—but really, it is not scary inasmuch as it is beyond my control. I am vulnerable. Fear is the carnal response. Vulnerability is the spiritual response.

I'm looking forward to seeing how God will work this out for my good and move us to new territory.

* * *

Exhale
Baby, it's just the beginning
Christ in you
Won it all
Take a step back
Look at all your forward movement
Progress. Potential. Poised
Deep breath inward
Slowly release
Keep moving forward
Keep grinding it out
Being certain to rest

I'm vulnerable in His presence
Knowing what I know
There's no telling
Where I'll go
Deep fashion
Walking on the sea
There is no limit
To the Christ in me
Exhale

* * *

Now is the appointed time. I struggled when God told me to end this book with "the appointed time"—I thought it was the same as the beginning. But it is not.

The beginning is when a thing starts; the appointed time is the best time—the set time—for a thing to happen.

Kairos is now.

I can be all that God created me to be. And now, in history, is the time for my assignment to be fulfilled. All that Satan tried to do to abort my mission on earth has failed. From convincing me that I was crazy to turning my child against me to vex my soul— I have survived.

The Holy Spirit says: "Breaking into destiny and breaking out of fear will require a specific push from God. The anointing destroys the yoke. When I push you, what is in you will rise up and take care of the situation. You will not fall or fail, but rise."

I was being vulnerable and being pushed. Initially, I braced myself for the PUSH. I only imagined it could be devastating pain, something catastrophic, heartbreaking, or earth-shattering—maybe.

But bracing myself isn't what my anatomy is made of. I have great vulnerability. I can be vulnerable and pushed. Like a child on a swing. I will rise.

This is the opportune time to see God shine in His glory through me. There is a divine reason fear is time-stamped, and its expiration date has passed.

I'm called into ministry. And what I couldn't say earlier for fear is —I'm called as one of God's prophets. I'm also called to preach and teach. I'm a leader and a minister. I'm appointed to pray and lay hands on the sick—to see souls saved and others healed. I am a witness. I follow in the footsteps of Jesus, taking up my cross and following Him.

The burden is real, but so is the advancement of the kingdom. It's time for God to get all the glory. This is my story. This is my anatomy. I am a warrior for Christ, vulnerably.

And so she moved. On a word from the Lord.

Facing her fears
Facing giants from her past
Facing demons in her present
Facing systems
But most of all—she was facing God and herself

According to Oxford Languages, anatomy is *"a study of the struc-ture or internal workings of something."*

What was working in her was vulnerability. It empowered her to face giants, demons, systems, God, and herself. This was the only way forward. And it was the opportune time for it to occur.

"Something is happening inside of me," she said. As I think on the word anatomy, I realize that God is showing me who I am—what I am made of. And in knowing me I can know who He is.

Simultaneously, He's showing me His relentless pursuit of me—His undying love for me—how He died to reveal that love.

Another definition for anatomy focuses more on science and the study of humans, plants, and animals, revealing their parts. That is exactly what God is doing. *Yes!*

With pain, disappointment, waiting, trials, good times, revelations of my gifts, tests, divine appointments, words of knowledge and wisdom, and all sorts of wonders and signs.

When you are living in fear, you miss out on the wonder of it all. I say that because—here, God has been chasing me down with His love—breaking yokes and untying me from bondages in His pursuit—revealing who I am.

And yet, I was so deep in fear that all I could see was:

- The threats
- The evil
- The danger
- And what I didn't want to happen

All I could feel was the heartache.

When we think of the cross, we think of:

- The pain
- The agony
- The suffering of our Savior
- The evil that brought it about

But the love that kept Him there is greater. That is what is meant by: "Greater is He that is in us than he that is in this world."

The love is greater.
The anatomy of a warrior is love.
Vulnerable love.
What kept Jesus on the cross was love.
Perfect love.

My new prayer is what Jesus prayed in the Garden of Gethsemane just before He was crucified: "Thy will be done."

Prayer of Encouragement

God wants to heal you through my story, using my pain as a platform to display His grace and great love. Surrender is the vehicle, and a loving relationship with the Father, Son, and Holy Spirit is the destination.

May God heal every wound from betrayal—those backstabbing moments you never saw coming from the people you trusted as a child. May His perfect love teach you to trust again. May Jesus restore the perfect peace and harmony that come only from keeping your mind stayed on Him. May love be evident in both your actions and inactions.

May God be glorified through your life, even in the midst of pain and trials. May He teach you to trust Him through it all, as He shapes your character and reveals His power and lordship to the world. May all who witness your journey see and know that Jesus is Lord because of your testimony.

In the name of Jesus, Amen.

Acknowledgments

My God, my God, has been faithful. He has pursued me with an irresistible love, transforming my mind—about myself, about the world, and about what is possible. In moments of doubt, when I questioned Him and what He could do, He remained patient. He has gently revealed His character, not through condemnation, but through unfailing love. He has taught me how to love myself, how to be vulnerable in relationships, how to speak up, and how to truly listen. Oh, what a mighty God I serve. Oh, what a love that has found me. I came to Him broken, and He has made me whole.

Thank You, Lord, for being my Father, my Best Friend, my Husband. Thank You, Jesus, for being my Savior. Your blood covers my sin and shame, and because of You, I am free. I stand in right relationship with the Father because of You, Jesus. And thank You, Lord, for sending the Holy Spirit. I cannot imagine where I would be without His constant instruction, guidance, insight, leading, nudging, reminders, warnings, prophetic utterances, and encouragement. He is truly the Comforter and Advocate.

To my mom: I want to thank the Lord for blessing me with a praying mother like you. You have always been in my corner—my number one cheerleader. As a single parent raising two children, you gave your all and then some. You took me to church as a child and set a godly example through the way you carried yourself with grace and dignity. I didn't realize how rare that was until I got older and saw that not every young girl had a role model like you. You were always giving, always going the extra mile—especially during the times when I struggled with mental illness and addiction. Mom, thank you for your giving heart. Thank you for keeping our family connected and for instituting family prayer.

To my Aunt Angel: Thank you for always having my back. No matter what season of life I was in, when I needed help, you were there. You are always so thoughtful, always giving, always blessing others. Thank you for your godly example—serving in ministry without a title, simply doing the Lord's work. You have taught me what it means to serve humbly and to love others well.

To my Cousin Porsha: We grew up like sisters, but drifted apart. I never imagined we'd reconnect the way we have, but God's hand was at work. You are now my sister in Christ, and I am so grateful for your prayers, encouragement, and the way God uses you in my life. The transformation He has done in you is nothing short of a miracle, and I am honored to be your cousin.

To my little brother, Earl: I love you. Thank you for always telling me I could do better and be better—even when I didn't believe you. I finally see what you saw in me all along. You have always been a dreamer, confident in your purpose and vision. I pray that God reignites that fire in you, that you dream again, and that you walk boldly into all He has for you.

To my Uncle Donnie: You are faithful, loyal, and kind. Thank you for being a wonderful uncle to me. In my toughest moments, when I felt backed into a corner, you showed up—time and time again. I pray that God grants you the desires of your heart.

To Kamani: Your spirit is amazing. I admire the way you support Porsha and the father you are. Your kindness and warmth never go unnoticed. Every time I came over for an event, you welcomed me with love, always smiling. I know life isn't always easy, but you still find a way to show love. Thank you for that, Kamani.

To Alexyus: You are a warrior—a prayer warrior, a strong and special young lady. Thank you for being you. Thank you for being an incredible big sister to KJ and Ari. I admire your dedication to school, swimming, and learning new languages. But more than anything, I am proud of you for knowing that your worth is not in what you do but in who you are—loved.

About the Author

I'm weak. The things I used to hide behind—my intellect, ministry work, and achievements—mean nothing (Philippians 3:7).

Oftentimes, I feel lost and unqualified. I get anxious and scared. I once thought God only wanted to see my good side, so I hid my humanity from Him. But He is my good side. And my weakness? His strength is made perfect in it (2 Corinthians 12:8-10).

I surrender the facade. I stop pretending I can hold it all together. Everything I've accomplished in my 40 years—I dare not boast in any of it, except that Jesus Christ was with me, growing me, pursuing me, and making it all possible.

www.ingramcontent.com/pod-product-compliance
Lightning Source LLC
Chambersburg PA
CBHW051241120626
46547CB00014B/1737